JEEP WRANGLER

THE STORY BEHIND AN ICONIC OFF-ROADER

NIGEL FRYATT

AMBERLEY

First published 2017

Amberley Publishing
The Hill, Stroud,
Gloucestershire, GL5 4EP

www.amberley-books.com

Copyright © Nigel Fryatt, 2017

The right of Nigel Fryatt to be identified as the Author
of this work has been asserted in accordance with the
Copyright, Designs and Patents Act 1988.

ISBN 978 1 4456 7137 6 (print)
ISBN 978 1 4456 7138 3 (ebook)

British Library Cataloguing in Publication Data.
A catalogue record for this book is available from the British Library.

Typeset in 10pt on 13pt Celeste.
Origination by Amberley Publishing.
Printed in the UK.

Contents

	Foreword	5
Chapter 1	Attention! Military Demands Produce an Off-Road Icon	7
Chapter 2	Changing Partners, but not the Philosophy	20
Chapter 3	The Wrangler Range: Peace Arrives, and the Wrangler is Born	27
Chapter 4	Mods and Rockers: Anything Goes as Long as it's Different	53
Chapter 5	Concept Vehicles: Looking to the Future, and the Past	67
Chapter 6	Buy It, Use It: The Best Way to Enjoy the Wrangler	84

Foreword

Jeep Wrangler: An Off-Road Icon

The Jeep Wrangler is a very special vehicle, fully deserving its very own book. From a difficult and uncompromising beginning, and surviving some major turbulent changes in ownership over the years, it remains a vehicle that is developing, changing and progressing. What is obvious, however, is the heritage that has seeped into every nut and bolt. We have described it as an iconic off-roader, and we don't use that word lightly; it's a very special vehicle.

Over the years I have been very lucky to drive a variety of Jeep products, and not just the Wrangler. However, it's fair to say that it's this model that has given the most enjoyment, especially when off-road. You cannot fail to drive a Wrangler in the rough and not have a smile on your face, and so producing this book has been a pleasure. Of course, it could not be done without the help of many people and the list is really too long to mention here, but I do have to say thanks to Tom Johnson in the Press & PR Department of Fiat Chrysler Automobiles UK, who thankfully always seems to recognise exactly what a journalist needs. Cheers Tom. A big thanks also to Sue Loy, who has had the thankless task of proofreading my copy; thankfully, Sue also shares my enthusiasm for the Jeep brand.

All that's left is for me to let you read the book, and enjoy the many pictures that we have collected. If you are a Jeep Wrangler owner, I hope there's something in here that you didn't know, and if you are new to the Jeep range, I certainly hope it makes you consider a Wrangler. It's not often that you can buy an icon, and then take it off-road and cross terrain other vehicles would have to avoid. Long live the Jeep Wrangler.

Nigel Fryatt
April 2017

Many thanks must also go to all those who kindly supplied photographs. The majority are from company press and publicity departments, but a selection are from individuals, and without these, the books would be much diminished. A final 'thanks' has to go a good friend, respected journalist and dedicated Jeep enthusiast Bob Cooke. I have learnt more about Jeeps from Bob than any other expert; sadly he passed away before I was able to show him this book, but I am pleased that he is included, photographed driving in his inimitable style on page 11.

CHAPTER 1

Attention! Military Demands Produce an Off-Road Icon

Designed to be a light reconnaissance vehicle with the ability to go almost anywhere, the military Jeep is the true ancestor to the Wrangler.

The story of the Jeep Wrangler goes back a very long way, and to a very different time. Some forty-seven years before the first Jeep to carry the Wrangler name was launched, the world was involved in its second global conflict, and by 1940 the likelihood that the United States of America would be joining the Second World War in Europe was growing with the arrival of every news bulletin. Such a situation concentrated the minds of many, and the US military was no exception. While the motorised tank had entered the First World War, the main method of transport for any army had been the horse; it transported individuals, pulled supply wagons and dragged guns and ammunition through the mud that would defeat many of the bigger commercial trucks used. The US Army had been experimenting with motorised military options throughout the 1920s and 1930s, primarily producing four-wheel drive versions of existing commercial vehicles. The US military believed, however, that there was an urgent need for a light and practical reconnaissance vehicle that could travel across difficult terrain. It needed to be simple to build, cheap and, most importantly, it needed to be easy to repair when on the front line. Perhaps the most stringent demand, however, was that the US military wanted it 'yesterday'.

The wonderfully named American Quartermaster Corps Technical Committee released a specific set of requirements in 1940, inviting motor manufacturers to produce prototype models. These requirements were specific and the extremely tight timetable meant that there were not many manufacturers prepared to even attempt the proposal. It is no surprise, therefore, that of all the US automakers at the time, only two relatively small companies responded: the American Bantam Car Company of Butler, Pennsylvania, and Willys-Overland of Toledo, Ohio. Ford merely sent an observer, but this was to prove highly significant.

History has a tendency to review a glorious patriotic success through rose-tinted spectacles, but the story goes that the original design was conceived over a weekend by a young Detroit engineer called Karl K. Probst. Bear in mind that his design would have been on paper, using pencils, a slide rule and, as you might expect, a particularly large eraser. He produced a design for a vehicle that would have a top speed of 55 mph (which may sound rather limited today, but in 1940 was reasonably fleet of foot), was able to wade through water up to 18 inches deep, could carry a payload of 360 kg and had a mounting that could carry a .30 calibre machine gun. To top this off, it was to weigh only 1,000 kg, which made it light enough for men to lift the whole vehicle out of a ditch if necessary – he even designed 'grab handles' on the vehicle's sides to make this possible. Whether any GIs, deep in conflict during the Second World War, ever thanked Karl K. Probst for adding those handles, however, has never been recorded...

The US military's top brass were impressed with the initial design and gave Bantam a contract to build some seventy prototypes, and these models impressed everyone during the first test carried out in September 1940. The US Army did, however, have reservations, thinking that as Bantam was such a small company, it would not be able to produce the vehicle in the numbers required in the time available. Because of this, Willys-Overland and Ford were asked to bid to build their own versions, but using Probst's basic designs.

The Willys option had the more powerful engine – the wonderfully named 'Go-Devil' unit, with its 6.5:1 compression ratio making it easy to start and deliver its impressive 60 hp. Ford produced a vehicle of better craftsmanship, due to their greater experience in mass-production. Bantam, still hoping it would get the final nod for production, updated its vehicle, producing the lightest and most fuel efficient of the three. Unfortunately for Bantam, it was Willys and Ford that got the final contracts and, perhaps ironically, Bantam was reduced to designing and building a trailer to be pulled behind the new Willys and Ford models.

Records now suggest that over 637,000 of these original Jeeps were built and served in the Second World War, with many finding themselves travelling all over the globe, across Europe, through the deserts of North Africa, the jungles of the Pacific and throughout Asia. After the war, a few even made it all the way to Japan and were the inspiration for the growth of the off-roaders from the likes of Mitsubishi, Suzuki and Toyota; but that's another story for another time, and another book! The Willys-built models were known as the MB, for Model B, and the Ford options were the GPWs, for General Purpose Willys. The military just described the vehicle as 'a Truck, ¼-ton, 4x4'.

Willys Overland's prototype for the US Army contract was the Quad, which was fitted with the Go-Devil side-valve four-cylinder engine.

Even this very early Willys MA has certain design features that Jeep enthusiasts the world over can recognise.

How many servicemen can you get into a Jeep? As many as necessary, would be the official answer.

The horse had always been the 'vehicle' of choice. The Jeep changed all that; this is a Ford GP version.

Star of stage and screen, this Willys Jeep, affectionately known as *Elusive Elaine*, has appeared in numerous UK film and television productions.

Elusive Elaine meets up with a 2011 model year Wrangler. The heritage is obvious.

The driver sat on the fuel tank, but then most drivers had worse things to worry about...

No one is denying that the original design is a long way from today's Wrangler, yet you only have to look at the slotted front grille and headlights of Probst's first design to see the link with today's Jeep model range. Indeed, that very design is now used by Jeep to reinforce its brand and can be clearly seen across its model range.

Driving a Legend

Today, early Second World War Jeeps are not only in demand from military vehicle enthusiasts, but also film directors! These days, many people's first exposure to the Jeep will have been on the big screen, with John Wayne, Ronald Reagan or even the entire cast of cult film MASH behind the wheel. Reliable, authentic Jeep models are in much demand for film and TV work and in the UK one of the 'stars' you are likely to have seen is known affectionately as *Elusive Elaine* (as with fighter planes and bombers, many Second World War Jeeps were given female names and illustrated motifs).

Getting behind the wheel of *Elaine* is an intriguing experience. Obviously, since it has no doors, you feel very open and vulnerable, an emotion strengthened by the fact that these vehicles were built purely to be used in conflict. She's a Willys Jeep, fitted with that famous Go-Devil engine and when this author was lucky enough to sit behind the driving wheel, it started the first time and ran surprisingly smoothly. You snick first gear by pulling back and down (where you would expect second on a normal modern vehicle) and the 2.2 litre engine bounds forward like an enthusiastic pet dog. Rough gravel climbs, deep mudded ruts, humps and bumps are all covered with ease and you can quickly appreciate just how the US top brass must have felt at those first test drives. The Jeep appears unstoppable – an impression further enhanced when you realise just how hard you need to stamp on the brake to get the brake shoes to contact with the drums (disc brakes were still many years away for modern vehicles); perhaps it would have been helped by wearing authentic US Army specification boots!

The most important technical aspect of the original military Jeep, and one that of course continues to the present-day Wrangler, is that both are four-wheel drive. Even in 1940 the benefits of driving all the wheels were appreciated, although perhaps all the difficulties that this can create were not. For the original Willys, the system is operated by two separate levers, positioned just to the right of the gear lever. You simply pull the larger lever back and this engages drive to the front axle (for 'normal' driving on firm dry roads the Jeep would remain in two-wheel drive, as many modern SUVs do today). The smaller lever engages the low ratio part of the gearbox to aid the Jeep when the conditions got really tough. Interestingly, there's a lock mechanism that prevents low range being selected when the Jeep is only in two-wheel drive, since doing so would probably destroy the gearbox. It was accepted that conflict conditions were going to prevent much advance driver training for military personal, so making Jeeps as 'idiot proof' as possible was necessary. Today, while the systems in modern Wranglers are more sophisticated, the principle is the same; if you have a manual Wrangler, there is a set process needed to select four-wheel drive first, and then low range. More modern electronic systems and automatic gearboxes take much of the decision process away from the driver, but the principle remains.

Versions were made to cope with all conditions; this is the Jeep Snow Tractor, complete with front wheel skis.

13

The Willys MT-Tug 6x6 was designed to carry increased payload; in particular, a very large gun.

Come fly with Jeep. It is claimed that this crazy machine did actually get airborne, but it was never put into production.

Ford built a large number of amphibious Jeeps, known as Seeps, although they were not that successful in getting out of the water. (Historical images courtesy of Mark Askew. For more information on military Jeeps, check out www.jeepworld. co.uk)

Limited numbers of the Willys MA were made. This one is shown as being capable of pulling significant artillery.

The Ford GPW was built in greater numbers, with some 277,896 having been produced.

The design also proved amazingly flexible. Quite apart from carrying five-star generals and lowly privates to and from the front line, Jeeps could be fitted with machine guns, or trail larger artillery cannons, or were used as ambulances. Jeeps were modified to run with caterpillar tracks, like tanks, and they were made to be able to float across rivers; there was even one version fitted with a rotary engine to lift the Jeep like a helicopter. The Rotabuggy Flying Jeep did, apparently, make it into the air, but the project was soon abandoned when it was realised that actually it made more sense to build bigger cargo planes and fit Jeeps into them! The versatility and flexibility of the original design does, however, point the way to the future, and especially to the Jeep Wrangler.

Even today, if you are lucky enough to drive a working Willys Jeep, you will be impressed by its abilities over rough terrain, and the ease with which you can drive it. Drive an early Jeep and a more modern Wrangler, and while one will be somewhat more comfortable, and may even have a roof and doors, the heritage is obvious. It's unlikely that the Wrangler as we know it today would exist without this early Jeep. It may seem odd to say so, but all Wrangler enthusiasts can thank the very special demands created by the Second World War for the existence of their favourite Jeep. But there is still a big gap to close; how did we get from a basic, sparse, military reconnaissance vehicle, to the high-quality leisure 4x4 we have today?

The Jeep had obviously proved its abilities in a tough environment, and it was logical that Willys executives should want to consider a peacetime production of post-war models. Originally, they didn't make many changes, merely improving the headlights (you needed

The Civilian Jeeps started in 1945 with the CJ-2A. Initially, it remained with the 60 hp Go Devil engine of its military cousin.

This CJ-5 has the original factory hardtop, extending its versatility. Note the sliding doors.

to see where you were going and as opposed to a war situation, it was good if people could also see you), making the seats were more comfortable (soldiers could complain it was uncomfortable and it wouldn't matter, private paying customers were different), and they fitted a rear tailgate to improve the ability to carry loads.

The first peacetime model was the Willys CJ-2A. Later, in 1942, came a Station Wagon version and in 1947 there was the first Jeep pickup – a model that is important, as 2018 will see the introduction of a new Jeep Wrangler pickup.

Initially, in the aftermath of the war, most of the contracts for new models were from military sources and this was a global market. In an age long before the Internet and mass global marketing campaigns, Willys, however, had a wonderfully simple marketing campaign, all thanks to the US military. When the war was over and the US troops came home, the majority of the Jeeps were just left behind. This was delightfully described by Patrick Foster, author of the excellent book *Jeep: The History of America's Greatest Vehicle,* as 'the ultimate free sample'.

It was these free samples that helped to grow the Jeep's reputation when hostilities ended, and to bolster overseas sales. Closer to home, the end of the war saw the returning troops well versed in the vehicle's abilities, and with the growing optimism of the 1950s and '60s, the growth in leisure culture and the extensive opportunities to go hunting, shooting and fishing throughout America's vast, highly attractive countryside, so grew the need for a privately owned machine that could get you there. If its origins had been due to the demands of war, it was the consumer demand to enjoy our free time that turned that original design into a successful range of off-road vehicles that led us to the Jeep Wrangler of today.

After the war, models like this Willys MB were reconfigured for civilian use, often for agricultural purposes.

Today, Jeep reunions are highly popular. This picture comes from the famous Goodwood Revival meeting.

An early advertisement. It is interesting to note that when the military versions were first made available for civilians, it was via Willys dealers, and the name Jeep appears as 'Jeep'.

Where Did the Name Come From?

Quite where the name 'Jeep' came from has been much discussed over the years, and to be honest no one can be completely sure. The idea that Second World War GIs created the nickname as some of the original models from Ford were known as GPs (General Purpose) can really be dismissed, since only the Ford models were GPs. What about the Willys MBs? It is also claimed that American service personnel in the First World War generally called various military planes and vehicles 'jeeps'. Soldiers in Korea are said to have called it the Jeep as it had 'Just Enough Essential Parts'.

But if you are looking for a more colourful and entertaining 'answer', then we prefer the version that says the word comes from the rather fantastical character that appeared in Popeye comics that date back to the 1930s. For those unfamiliar with Popeye, he was one of the first superheroes, a committed vegetarian, and a righter of wrongs, especially when those wrongs were directed towards his stick-thin girlfriend Olive Oyl. In these stories, writer E. C. Segar included a rather strange yellow-spotted 'pet' to the story, called Eugene the Jeep. Besides having a large and oddly coloured proboscis, Eugene only every said 'jeep', but he had remarkable magical powers that allowed him to 'go anywhere and do anything' – attributes that are exactly what the manufacturer would want for its new civilian off-roader. That's the story this writer prefers; 'jeep, jeep'.

CHAPTER 2

Changing Partners, but not the Philosophy

The success that the Jeep Wrangler enjoys today has come at a price and emanates from an extraordinary international industrial story that is both complex and at times somewhat surprising. Indeed, the Jeep brand appears to have been bought and sold like an unloved used car, with ownership swinging across the Atlantic and back no less than three times. Some owners have been close to financial ruin and US Presidents have been directly involved with the brand's future, with Jeep being finally rescued by the Italians, which, given the brand's original conception, has to be something of a magnificent irony.

Once the Second World War was over, and peacetime manufacturing in the United States got underway, it was motor manufacturing that was to be among the most vibrant. Companies grew as demands rose and numerous smaller manufacturers were bought, sold and merged by bigger, more aggressive rivals. In 1953, Willys-Overland was purchased by the Kaiser Manufacturing Company, which dropped the 'Overland' and added 'Motors'. It was ten years later that the Willys name disappeared completely and for the first time the word Jeep appeared, with the creation of the Kaiser-Jeep Company.

The Jeep Toledo plant in 1964, with CJ models being produced alongside station wagons. Note the wooden factory flooring.

This is the Willys-Overland Forge shop, which was photographed in 1916.

Compared to today's modern facilities, this 1916 shot of the Willys-Overland production facility shows how basic and brutal vehicle production was at the time.

A mere six years later, in 1963, American Motors acquired Kaiser-Jeep, but all was not well with AMC's finances at the time. With the benefit of hindsight, it is easy to see why, when you look at the models the company were producing at the time! Jeep must have looked like a life-saver; an established brand with a strong, enthusiastic, albeit rather small, customer base, but it was not to be and in 1978 Renault took a 25 per cent stockholding in AMC. The French company could see that Jeep was the strong part of the company, and when the new Cherokee model was launched in 1984, it was Renault that brought it over to Europe. It was a landmark vehicle in that it was a monocoque construction SUV, with an elegant design and excellent off-road abilities, but if you wanted to buy this American-built Jeep in Europe, you went to a French Renault dealership; odd, and not particularly successful.

So, in a relatively short time, when measured against the usual timescale of corporate life, Jeep had started at Bantam (a company deemed as not big enough to produce its own successful design), before moving to Willys, which was bought and then sold by Kaiser to

AMC (a company that needed French finance from Renault to move forward). In America, commentators even spoke of the 'Jeep Curse' to describe what was happening, since it seemed that Jeep was the common denominator with all these issues. Thankfully, one man saw the Jeep brand as anything but a curse.

Lee Iacocca was a particularly dynamic US motor industry executive, who is often remembered for his part in the development of the all-American sports car, the Ford Mustang. After Ford, he was persuaded to head up the American giant Chrysler – a company that at the time can best be described as 'slumbering'. Despite financial challenges, Iacocca revitalised Chrysler and one of the ways he did this was to buy the Jeep brand from AMC. It was the profitable part of AMC, so it probably took some careful negotiating; but then, AMC also needed the money!

It was a shrewd move, and Chrysler was a good place for the development of the Jeep brand. The Cherokee was a big success and they introduced the upmarket Grand Cherokee in 1992. The Wrangler, though smaller in actual sales numbers, had been developed over the years and represented the real essence of the Jeep brand.

A growing global player, Chrysler was then courted by the German carmaker Daimler and a merger was agreed. Profitability was good at this time, and this led to a significant upgrade in the Toledo manufacturing plants, which in turn led to the development of the four-door Wrangler Unlimited. If this is a plus in the story, Daimler also influenced Jeep models like the Compass and Patriot, which may have had a Jeep badge on the famous seven-slot front grille, but were not true tough off-roaders, as customers were quick to comment. Daimler was also concerned that the then cheaper but still relatively luxurious Grand Cherokee was undermining its Mercedes-Benz brand in some market areas, which led to decisions being made about the Jeep Grand Cherokee that did little to help sales. It was an unsatisfactory alliance and eventually the two companies decided to 'unmerge', with the costs being paid for by Daimler. Now on its own, however, Chrysler struggled in the US, and this began to affect the Jeep brand. In the UK, Jeep dealerships faded away and sales plummeted. It was feared by some that the brand would disappear forever. Was the 'Jeep Curse' finally to kill this famous off-road brand?

When taking over Chrysler Jeep after the 2009 financial crisis, the US President at the time, Barrack Obama, had a lot to thank Fiat's CEO Sergio Marchionne for.

The one millionth Wrangler rolled off the Toledo production line in the summer of 2013; a black Wrangler Rubicon 10th Anniversary Edition.

The separate chassis and engine meets the Wrangler bodyshell for the first time, in what is often described as the 'marriage'.

The Wrangler has all its hydraulic fluids filled up with the help of a giant robotic arm.

23

Employees secure the front facia to the Wrangler; the famous seven-slot front grille is instantly recognisable.

Standing alone, however, the Jeep Wrangler remained a strong model; sales were small overseas, but were strong in the US, and the bigger four-door Unlimited version had been well received and increased its market to become a family fun off-roader. The bigger problem, however, was that Chrysler's bread-and-butter models did not have such demand. Add to that the global financial 'credit crunch', and in 2009 Chrysler sought bankruptcy protection from the US Government. President Obama couldn't let Chrysler fail, since it had a significant workforce, being the number three US carmaker at the time, and he didn't want to lose those jobs.

Once again, the saviour came from the other side of the Atlantic in the surprising shape of Fiat SpA, a company that was not particularly successful in Europe at the time, but was led by a forward-thinking CEO by the name of Sergio Marchionne. Like others before him, Marchionne saw the potential of the Jeep brand. He also saw a way of getting the Fiat brand to sell in the United States and, to top it all, he saw a company, and a US president, ready to do a deal.

Fiat's acquisition of the Jeep brand surprised many commentators, and would continue to surprise for the next couple of years. Climbing out of the global recession, Fiat has injected some much-needed life into the brand. The top-of-the-range Grand Cherokee has been significantly improved and a brand-new Cherokee has been built in the US, based on a Fiat platform. An important new sub-compact, the Jeep Renegade, has been produced. This is a name that is familiar to Jeep enthusiasts, but not so familiar is the fact that it is built at Melfi in southern Italy, and it is the first Jeep to be imported into the US. The model has received deserved praise and sales have been strong, all of which is big a bonus for the Wrangler.

A sign for the future: this is a Jeep Renegade being built at Fiat's Melfi plant in southern Italy. This is the first Jeep to be built outside the US and then exported back to be sold in the home country.

Wranglers all receive numerous checks when complete, before they leave the production line and head off to dealer showrooms.

Building a Wrangler is a complex procedure, and still involves humans rather than just robots.

In 2016, Jeep celebrated its 75th Anniversary – something that hadn't looked likely on numerous occasions during its troubled history – and through all this, the Jeep Wrangler managed to remain the very heart of a model range that had chopped and changed at the whims of its different owners, but none of whom had, thankfully, tried to change the Wrangler. 2018 will see a completely new model, one that will be lightyears away from that original Bantam design. It will have its own range, including a new pickup version. While there have been independently produced Wrangler pickup conversions before, this will be an official mass-produced version, with a heritage that can be traced back to a 1947 truck version.

At the time of writing this book, global sales of Jeep products are strong, the model range is impressive and the plans from Fiat, which are looking towards the future, deserve to succeed. The Jeep Wrangler continues to develop, to sell, to provide entertainment for its owners. Yet, despite all this good news, you can't help but wonder, with a history of seemingly unsuitable owners and fragile financial confidence, whether the story is really over. As we were completing this book, respected US motor trade publication *Automotive News* reported that Chinese manufacturer Great Wall was 'deeply interested' in buying the Jeep brand. Whether that will happen given the politics of today is questionable, but it rear forces the fact that the brand has a truly global appeal!

Above: The giant 'rock' logo outside the Toledo production facility. The Wrangler looks tiny in its presence.

Left: The front entrance to the Ohio factory. This new assembly complex was built on the site of the original Stickney Plant.

Chapter 3

The Wrangler Range: Peace Arrives, and the Wrangler is Born

The development of the Jeep range after the Second World War was a cautious affair. This was probably because the manufacturer was unaware at the time of exactly what the public really wanted from the vehicle; this was indeed a completely new area for private vehicle production, and therefore it was difficult to estimate demand.

Initially, therefore, the CJ models – 'Civilian Jeep' – followed the developments for the military versions closely. The differences for private customers were limited to things like seat padding, lighting and the fact that some new funky colours were used, rather than the usual rather drab olive green. The need was no longer to camouflage the vehicle – now you wanted everyone to see you!

The CJ-3A model arrived in 1949 with a reworked front windscreen, but it took four years before there was a significant change, which occurred when the more powerful Willys Hurricane engine was fitted in the CJ-3B. The engine's size meant that the bonnet line had to be raised, thereby changing the actual profile of the Jeep. But it wasn't until 1955 when the CJ-5 was released that you can really see the shape and basic specification that was to become the hallmark of the Jeep range, and was to continue (albeit with a multitude of modifications) up to the present-day Wrangler range.

The CJ model range ran for nearly forty years and it was this success, and the enthusiasm of customers, that made the company consider a replacement, leading to the introduction of the Wrangler.

The original CJ-2A started in 1945. Note the folded windscreen and the rather odd location of the spare wheel.

It was actually commercial demands that made the CJ series such a success. This is a long-wheelbase version, and yet is still a two-door.

A Jeep Dispatcher 100, built in 1974 during the company's ownership by AMC. Note it is right-hand drive, so the postman could deliver to US mailboxes without getting out of the vehicle.

In case you are wondering, there was indeed a CJ-4. At the time, there were many licensing agreements for overseas companies to build their own versions of the CJ range – Mitsubishi in Japan and Spanish-built Viasa and Ebro models were a couple of the most important. In India, the CJ-3B was licensed to Mahindra & Mahindra, where there was a demand for more interior space. An agreement was made to allow Mahindra & Mahindra to produce extended-wheelbase versions to create the CJ-4. This model actually predates Jeep's Toledo factory's own long-wheelbase CJ-6 version, and is quite often a 'forgotten' model.

The CJ-5 followed, and for many enthusiasts this model is the heart stone of the classic Jeep. The body was smoothed and almost streamlined, with the rounding of the bonnet edges and the larger, downward-pointing front bumpers (to stop the older model's trait of throwing mud into the driver's face). At the time, the US company described the model as being 'completely new' and indeed it gained new seats, a dashboard, a handbrake and much improved suspension. Under the bonnet, however, the venerable four-cylinder Hurricane engine remained, although the head was reworked and power was increased to a claimed 75 bhp. Originally fitted with the existing robust three-speed transmission, in 1968 an all-synchromesh three-speed became available, which was a major refinement and a step away from the model's military past. Few of these models remain in their original format these days, as the Jeep was just the sort of vehicle that enthusiasts could modify and customise – a trait that many owners took up with great enthusiasm.

This desire for personalisation was a marketing tool also recognised by the manufacturer, and to meet an owner's desire to be different and to 'be a free spirit', 1974 saw the first Renegade model, now with a more powerful V6 engine under the bonnet. Remember, this was the time when petrol prices in the US were low and fuel consumption was not an important consideration, whereas size – in this case cubic inches – was much more important and attractive to the buyer. The result was the V8-engined Renegade II, which arrived the following year. This 5 litre engine produced 150 bhp, and thanks to its thirst, a larger fuel tank had to be fitted.

For many enthusiasts, the CJ-5 is still the model that truly resembles exactly what Jeep means.

The first Renegade
model was actually
introduced in 1974,
with the more
powerful V6 engine.

The CJ Renegade
began the style of
personalisation;
bucket-style seating,
big wheels and tyres,
plus large bonnet
lettering.

Cheap petrol prices at
the time made fitting
a larger engine to this
model an easy decision
for the manufacturer
to make.

Fitted with the factory hardtop, the Jeep CJ range increased its market to places in the world where the sun doesn't shine every day.

The Jeep Scrambler was introduced in the 1980s, combining the Jeep's character with American's love of pickup trucks.

The CJ-5 was replaced in 1983 and the market was able to enjoy the CJ-7, which would carry the Laredo name proudly on its bonnet. There had been a CJ-6 version available, and this was the 20-inch longer-wheelbase version – the majority being used for commercial purposes – but it was the CJ-7 models that caught the imagination; popular throughout the US, these models also started to have an important following among European off-road enthusiasts. There were a number of significant modifications over the previous model, and probably one of the most important was the availability of an optional hardtop. Originally only available in black or white, this nevertheless made the open-topped fair weather machine into what the Americans called a 'compact station wagon'.

As with other CJ models, overseas licensing agreements led to some interesting variations. In Australia, for example, you could actually buy a CJ-7 fitted with a 2.4 litre Japanese Isuzu engine.

The final CJ model was logically the CJ-8, but it is more usually called the Jeep Scrambler. This longer-wheelbase version actually sold very well over its five-year production period and undoubtedly that success led to the eventual production of the larger four-door Unlimited Wrangler models.

The First Wrangler: YJ 1986–1996

In many ways, it is quite surprising that the CJ range continued for so long. It's true that it had been continuously developed and improved, but it was still basically that same spartan military machine produced to meet the demands of a nation at war. A production period of thirty-one years, therefore, is very impressive, but in 1986 the CJ was replaced with a new model, the Wrangler YJ, which made its debut at the 1986 Chicago Auto Show.

While the first Wrangler can justifiably claim to be a descendant of the original Jeeps, this was a completely new machine. Staunch Jeep traditionalists even started to call it the FJ Jeep, as in 'Freeway Jeep', as the model was now happy to cruise at speed on the tarmac, on American freeways. While this was meant to be a derogatory comment, it was a truism backed up by changing market demands. Back in the late 1970s, the majority of Jeep CJ owners did not use their machines every day; rather, they were for off-road fun and leisure options. By 1986, however, this had changed, and fewer people were taking them off-road and so, to ensure that sales increased, the Jeep Wrangler had to become more user-friendly when driven on the road; better roadholding and much improved steering were the necessary changes the public wanted.

Of course, it was important that it looked the part, and the YJ certainly carried all that was popular with previous models, but updated those traditional design markers and then added a lot more creature comforts. The Wrangler's ride height was lowered for better on-road driving and while some of the body panels directly reflected the CJ models, the Wrangler had a new purpose-built steel subframe and shared some components from the latest Cherokee model (another cause for complaint from those traditionalists).

When the Wrangler YJ was launched, it was designed for the street rather than the great outdoors.

The Cherokee association was especially evident with the decision to use the same rectangular headlamps (a decision that was changed when the replacement TJ arrived, as even Jeep recognised this was an error).

The model received the company's new Command Trac four-wheel drive system, which again aided in driving pleasure when on the road, but kept the traction necessary when off of it. Criticism would be directed towards the suspension, which remained leaf-sprung all round, limiting axle articulation. Interestingly, many owners improved this with simple suspension lifts, which raised the ride height and thereby increased that articulation and, in turn, the Wrangler YJ's off-road abilities.

Under the bonnet, owners had the option of a 2.5 litre four-cylinder or a 4.2 litre straight-six. Both produced around 120 hp, but the larger engine had a lot more low end torque and therefore tended to be the off-road option. A five-speed gearbox and the

The use of square headlights and an 'angled' front grille was an attempt to break from the model's CJ range, but they were not well received.

This 1990 Wrangler YJ sports one of the bright new colour schemes aimed at leisure owners.

In 1991, the Wrangler YJ Renegade arrived with the new 4.0 litre six-cylinder engine offering 180 hp.

With the benefit of hindsight, the YJ range is certainly not one of the best looking of Jeep's extensive heritage.

selectable Command Trac four-wheel drive system was standard. An automatic gearbox was not available until 1994, and was optional with the four-cylinder versions.

In 1991, the YJ became available with the then new 4.0 litre six-cylinder engine that offered a much improved 175 hp – a change that raised the vehicle's profile. In the UK, YJ models are relatively rare, although the ones that exist tend to be in good condition thanks to the fact that the body panels were galvanised and the model was protected against corrosion; thankfully, the manufacturer recognised that not all Jeep owners lived in a perfect Californian climate!

Production of the YJ was initially at the Brampton plant, in Ontario, Canada. This facility was actually closed in 1992 and production was moved to Toledo, Ohio. Interestingly, this was the same site that had built Willys Jeeps in the Second World War, but you would suspect that the production process would have changed somewhat! Toledo was to become the home of the Wrangler for its foreseeable future.

The Wrangler was an important export model for Jeep; this is a UK-spec 4.0 litre Sahara model.

In 1994, automatic transmission was made available for the smaller four-cylinder engine models.

The Wrangler Gets Serious: TJ 1996–2006

By 1990, Jeep was now in the hands of Chrysler and it was decided that the Wrangler was in need of an upgrade, and that it needed to offer better off-road ability to the market. The development of the Wrangler TJ took some time as the new owners wanted the second-generation Wrangler to be better in every area of performance, comfort, safety and, especially, off-road ability. As a result, the new model took some three years to be signed off, and the TJ made its debut at the Detroit Auto Show as a 1997 model year vehicle. It was the first Jeep model to be produced that was made available for both left- and right-hand drive markets from its launch, which indicated that the demand for the Wrangler was growing globally.

It was obvious as soon as it was unveiled that Chrysler designers had been listening to the traditional Jeep enthusiasts. Gone were the rectangular headlights and the slightly awkward 'bent' front grille; the new model proudly displayed the seven-slot upright grille and round headlights – pure Willys Jeep. It had an even

The upgraded Wrangler TJ immediately reasserted its position as a serious off-roader.

Changes for the TJ were significant, but, as ever, the Jeep's heritage and history was celebrated at the launch.

Gone were the horrible square headlamps and the angled front grille; the TJ has more in common with the CJ range than its predecessor.

more chunky and macho body shape, with more pronounced wheelarches, yet it remained unmistakably a Jeep.

Under that body, the Wrangler TJ got a version of the coil-sprung suspension that was being used on the Grand Cherokee, which certainly improved the vehicle's ride and handling. Whether this was in response to what Jeep's competitors were doing is difficult to say (Land Rover had been using coil springs since 1983), but whatever the reason, the new Quadra-Coil suspension was a significant change. Concerns about reckless drivers not appreciating the model's high stance and off-road abilities when thrashing the vehicle on the tarmac did lead to a slightly lower ride height than was probably needed, and yet despite this restriction, axle articulation was much improved over the YJ and offered the Wrangler TJ a much more compliant off-road ability. The previous model's leaf springs were capable, but led to a jolting 'crash and bang' progress over rough ground, while the new TJ gave the driver a more controlled off-road ride – something that drivers and passengers appreciated. It's a characteristic that has continued, and indeed improved, across the Wrangler range to the present day.

The familiar 4.0 litre six-cylinder engine, originating from Jeep's AMC days, powered most of the first TJ models, while a 2.5 litre four-cylinder remained available for the

Special edition TJs were all the rage; you just have to love a Wrangler Grizzly (not available in the UK).

The Jeep Wrangler won the 2002 4x4 Of The Year award from the UK's highly reputable *Off Road & 4 Wheel Drive* magazine.

entry level base models. In 2002, however, the newer 2.4 litre four-cylinder that had been launched in Chrysler's PT Cruiser was made available, raising the power to a more reasonable 140 bhp. Despite this new option, it's the 4.0 litre engine that is the one most enthusiasts chose, and would do today, even given the increased fuel consumption and the much-increased fuel prices since the launch.

Increased safety regulations saw the TJ now having both driver and passenger airbags, which in itself meant the need for a completely redesigned dashboard.

The Wrangler TJ is still the model of choice for many and prices in the UK today reflect the fact that you can now get a lot of Jeep for not a lot of money. Equipment and trim levels were relatively basic, but there has been a plethora of 'special editions' both in the US and in Europe. You could get a Sahara, Apex, Columbia, Freedom, Golden Eagle and Rocky Mountain, but our favourite just has to be the Wrangler Grizzly. One of the most valuable specials today was the model produced for the Jeep's 60th Anniversary in 2001; only two colours were available, but it looks great in either silver or black.

When the TJ arrived in the UK in 1997, it was aimed firmly at the sporting leisure market.

The interior was more 'car-like' than previous models, and its aim was to attract new buyers.

The Wrangler TJ, which is still thought by many to be the Wrangler that the true enthusiast wants to own.

The interior was spartan and very car-like, but that doesn't matter when you can remove the doors!

60th Anniversary Editions of the Jeep Wrangler TJ have become collector's models.

Other significant specials include the Tomb Raider model produced when the film *Lara Croft Tomb Raider: The Cradle of Life* was released in 2003. This was a limited run of 1,000, but it is thought that a few more than that were produced. Intriguingly, Jeep's off-road arch-rival, Land Rover, also had its own Lara Croft special version. Both the Wrangler and Land Rover versions have become highly collectable.

Good that it was in its standard format, off-road enthusiasts have created a demand for modifications that has seen an industry of aftermarket options to 'improve' your Wrangler (as we explain in a following chapter). For some, this remains *the* Wrangler to own – the best looking and still with the edge necessary to attract serious off-roaders. The initial reaction to the replacement JK model was, for some, a sign that the company had gone soft...

Present-Day Wranglers: JK 2007–2017

The third generation Wrangler began life during the difficult Daimler/Chrysler alliance, and while it was commissioned as early as 2001, the Wrangler JK wasn't unveiled until the 2006 North American Auto Show. This was a bigger Wrangler, it had grown in size and weight and led to some commentators describing the model as a 'bloated Yank tank'. Yet, while the new model was certainly bigger than its predecessor, the overall appearance didn't change that significantly. The JK retained the familiar round headlights, front grille and extended bumpers. It still had the familiar exposed door hinges and fold-down front windscreen. You could still remove the doors and that hardtop to replay that open, 'freedom' experience of the original Willys models.

The important changes were designed to increase the interior space for passengers and their luggage, demonstrated by the prominence of the four-door long-wheelbase Unlimited model, and it is certainly apparent when you get behind the wheel of the JK model that

This is why you own a Wrangler. The JK models offered comfort and class and the ability to leave the tarmac.

The new Wrangler JK models arrived in the UK for the 2007 model year.

The Sport is the base model of the JK range, yet still looks the business.

Original JK models had something of a basic, yet functional, interior. As the models have been updated, things have improved.

Open-air motoring is essential for Wrangler owners. The soft-top comes down easier than it goes back up...

Four fit in comfort, five at a squeeze. Note the integral roll bar speakers.

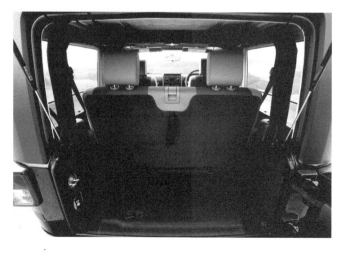

The camera's wide-angled lens rather implies there is a lot of rear luggage space. In truth, it is limited in the short-wheelbase model.

there is a lot more elbow room. The four-door offered the opportunity of taking the whole family on an adventure, although it has to be said that once you have four adults on board, additional luggage space is limited, especially in the short-wheelbase model. The longer-wheelbase Unlimited meant that the Wrangler's towing capacity increased from 1,000 kg for the two-door to 2,200 kg for the Sahara version and 2,000 kg for the Rubicon, giving the model moderate towing ability – certainly for the increasingly popular adventure trailers.

Right: This 2011 Wrangler shows that the company now offers some very funky colour options.

Below: Post 2011 Wranglers now have a much more opulent interior. The redesign raised the Wrangler's image and attracted new customers.

A UK launch shot of the then new JK range; once again, the original gets in on the act – this is a 1948 CJ-3A.

The longer, four-door Unlimited models have grown in popularity in the UK.

Those working in the wilds of the north in the UK recognise the benefits of the Wrangler.

Under this larger bodywork, the most significant changes were the engine variations. The options included the 2.8 litre turbodiesel from the Italian manufacturer VM Motori, which produced a welcome 174 bhp and a hefty amount of torque available from only 2,000 rpm (important for serious off-road driving). The top-of-the-range Rubicon came with the bigger 3.8 litre V6 petrol engine, which delivered an exciting 196 bhp. The Sport version was the base entry level Wrangler, with the Sahara being the mid-range option, which brought the benefits of an improved stereo system, Bluetooth connectivity and digital DAB radio; there was even the option of an integral satnav, and that's a long way from the communication versions of those original Willys Jeeps.

An unusual shot of the Wrangler without the roof, showing the comprehensive roll bar arrangement.

One of the benefits of the four-door Unlimited version is the increased luggage space.

This driver is wading his Wrangler perfectly; but this is not something you should do with the doors removed.

When crossing water, the entry is the important bit. This shot is close to the wading depth limit for the standard Wrangler.

The Wrangler was part of Jeep's 'Original Freedom' advertising campaign and this picture sums that up perfectly.

The pinnacle of the Wrangler range, at least as this book is being written, has to be the Rubicon version. For any serious off-roader, or indeed someone who wants the very best to compete in the urban jungle of the Tesco car park, this is the model for you. It comes with the larger, more powerful engine, but the important bits relate to the technical developments under the body. It has the top-of-the-range Command Trac four-wheel drive system, including the excellent Rock mode, which, when combined with Low Ratio, allows you to crawl your Wrangler up and over the most difficult of obstacles. Yes, a little driving skill is needed, and you will probably also need to have a 'spotter' outside the vehicle directing you where to go, but this Wrangler will do all the hard work and make you look like the complete off-road hero.

Above: The bonnet decals are back! The top-of-the-range Wrangler Unlimited Rubicon, complete with its Trail Rated badging.

Right: In 2017, the Jeep Wrangler won *4x4 Magazine's* 'Hardcore 4x4 Of The Year Award' for the third consecutive year.

Limited editions are still especially popular in the US. This is the Wrangler Polar.

The neat short-wheelbase Wrangler Islander special edition.

Just as those original civilian Jeeps after the Second World War were given fancy colours, so too are the modern versions.

Above: 2016 was the 75th anniversary of Jeep, and this is the Special Edition Wrangler, which is likely to become a collector's item.

Right: The official 75th Anniversary badging on all 2016 Wranglers and other Jeeps. It's a great design.

The Rubicon also has heavy-duty axles, with locking differentials, lower gearing, sill guards and bigger off-road tyres. It also has an electronic disconnect system for the sway bar (anti-roll bar). On the road, with the sway bar connected, the Wrangler Rubicon offers decent handling without the 'lean' that some tall off-road machines experience during enthusiastic driving and cornering. To facilitate this, the sway bar restricts wheel and body movement – great on tarmac, but not something you want when off road – so being able to disconnect at the touch of a button provides the significant bonus of being able to have the best of both worlds.

Later Wrangler JK models have an excellent Hill Descent Control, which allows the vehicle to crawl slowly down steep slopes, making any driver look like an off-road hero.

Remember that after you've been off-road, the engine bay may very well need a clean!

The badges say it all – this is what owning a Wrangler is all about; heritage, Trail Rated and unlimited enjoyment.

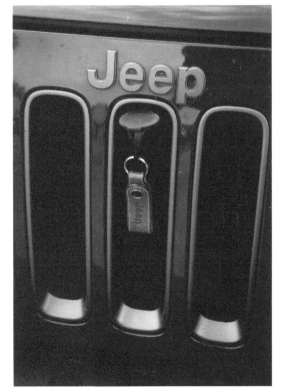

Above left: Neat design items are all over the Wrangler; this is the Jeep silhouette on the windscreen.

Above right: Large rubber clamps securely hold down the 2017 Jeep Wrangler's bonnet.

Right: Lock it up! All modern Jeep Wrangler bonnets are lockable using the vehicle's ignition key.

As the doors are removable, they have strong material straps.

If you are looking for the toughest Jeep models, always look for the Trail Rated badging. This is only given to the models in the Jeep range that the manufacturer has confirmed is capable of completing the famous Rubicon Trail through the Sierra Nevada in the western United States. For many off-roaders the world over, this is the Holy Grail when it comes to off-roading, and a Trail Rated Wrangler Rubicon was built for this challenge – literally.

When writing a book like this, you obviously have to stop when you come to the end of the story. With the Jeep Wrangler range, however, it is possible to look into our off-roading crystal ball. There will indeed be a fourth-generation Wrangler arriving in 2018. It will probably be more comfortable and more sophisticated than its predecessor. While owners of YJ, TJ and even the JK models will talk of the enjoyment of snicking the short, second gear lever into low range, it's likely that in future models much of this will be done by electronics and clever computers, and under the bonnet the engines will have become more fuel efficient to meet increasingly stringent environmental demands.

Nevertheless, while we can only surmise about what's coming, a number of things are certain; it will always look like a Jeep, its heritage from its impressive model range will be obvious, and it will be fun to drive both on, and off, the road.

Oh, and off the road will always be the best.

CHAPTER 4

Mods and Rockers: Anything Goes as Long as it's Different

If necessity is the mother of invention, then a vehicle that was conceived due to the demands of global conflict was always going to be simple to repair and rebuild. The rigours of a war scenario meant the original Jeeps had to be repairable not just with new spare parts, but also from components that could be salvaged from other Jeeps. This cannibalisation characteristic born under the strain and stress of battle situations emerged, in peacetime, as one reason why the Jeep became such a popular vehicle for off-road enthusiasts. There's nothing better than having a vehicle that you can customise, modify, improve, or just plain make 'different'. Early Jeeps offered exactly that, and when necessity of war turned into more peaceful customer enthusiasm, a massive industry was born that today means it is often difficult to find two Jeep Wranglers that are exactly the same!

A fully tricked-out Jeep Wrangler featuring many Rugged Ridge aftermarket products from Omix-ADA. Photograph courtesy of Rugged Ridge)

Above: Look carefully and you can still see the familiar Jeep grille and headlamps. This Wrangler racer is competing in the famous US King of the Hammers off-road racing event.

Left: Off-road racing US style means you need both speed and the ability to climb over rocks; note the massive front suspension strut.

Although there are still a reasonable number of early CJ models on the road, both in the US and throughout the rest of the world, it's difficult to find models that haven't been modified. The very fact that Willys and Ford originally built separate models, based on the same basic design, naturally lead to differences. Add to that the models that were produced under licence around the world after the war, and finding a completely original CJ can be difficult. As a result, prices for original Jeeps are certainly on the rise. For the American off-road enthusiast, however, the original enthusiasm wasn't about authenticity, it was all about getting out and enjoying your Jeep, and if that meant an engine swap or a suspension lift, all the better.

One particular aspect of this modification trend led to off-road racing, which, especially in the US, is now a highly professional affair with highly sophisticated, and expensive, racers being built that can tackle all terrains, at high speed and not break; well, not break that often. In the beginning, however, off-road racing was more of a hobby, and in the 1960s this involved enthusiasts taking their Jeeps to local club events. Starting in California, this quickly spread through states like Nevada and Arizona and it was Jeep that led the way. Today things are much more organised; the events are huge, the prize money is large but even at competitions like the famous US King of the Hammers competition, you'll still see the recognisable seven-slot grille and double headlamps on some competition machines, even if the rest of the vehicle has little in common with the production versions.

Above: The modification craze really took off with the TJ models. This is a nicely raised version from American Expedition Vehicles.

Right: Jeep recognised early the value of different model versions, hence the cute Jeepster Commando.

The Jeepster Commando was built on an extended-wheelbase CJ-6 model.

One of the first open-topped SUVs? The Jeepster Commando was certainly ahead of its time.

The flexibility of the Jeep range, even back in the 1960s, saw the then owners Kaiser-Willys respond to what the American marketing executives were calling the growth of 'Sports Utility Vehicles' (the origins of the SUV of today). As a result, Jeep decided to produce a model that was to compete with the very popular Ford Bronco. The Jeepster Commando was basically a rebodied long-wheelbase CJ-6 model, but with rear springs mounted on outriggers to improve the ride and handling. In total, there were four models available: a pickup, a station wagon, a convertible and a roofless roadster. It's easy to see from early promotional photographs exactly who the Jeepster Commando was aimed at – bright young things that spent all their time, it seemed, on the beach, wearing little clothing. Of course, this open-air SUV option has now been followed by Range Rover with its convertible Evoque model, so does this mean that Jeep got there some fifty years earlier? A good argument for the pub, perhaps.

The Jeepster was popular, and well received by the motoring media at the time. It also sold reasonably well, but was not a big enough commercial success to continue, especially when Jeep's ownership was set to change.

Lifting the suspension makes a big difference to the Wrangler. This mighty version has a suspension lift kit from Eibach. (Photograph courtesy of Eibach UK)

The SEMA Show takes place at Las Vegas and it's the place to go to see some amazing Jeep Wrangler conversions.

The best way to get a suspension lift is to go to the experts; this is the Eibach lift kit being fitted in the UK by Buzz Racing. (Photograph courtesy of Eibach UK)

Need a lift! This model was shown at the SEMA Show and was supported by the top aftermarket axle company Dana.

When the Wrangler YJ arrived in 1986, as we have explained in the previous chapter, it was aimed at a customer that would spend more time on the road than off it. As a result, the traditional semi-elliptic leaf springs had Panhard rods, firmly locating both axles and a front anti-roll bar to reduce body roll when cornering. This was good for tarmac driving, but it reduced the off-road ability. However, such was the Wrangler's following that many went back to that flexibility option we had seen in early models and tweaked their vehicles, often raising the suspension and greatly improving off-road ability. This trend grew, and with it so did the number of companies producing all the bits that an enthusiast could dream of. America was then, and remains, such a large market that the aftermarket product range quickly became both varied and high quality. Companies displayed their products at the annual Specialist Equipment Manufacturers Association (SEMA) Show that occurs in Las Vegas every year. Companies like American Expedition Vehicles (AEV), TeraFlex and Omix-ADA, with its Rugged Ridge range, now build whole 'new' Wranglers that are very different to those that roll off the Toledo production line. Omix-ADA claims to have a Jeep product line of some 20,000 parts, and a total stock worth a staggering $100 million. Some of the vehicles that AEV build are simply stunning, and the enthusiasm and sales success for that company's impressive Wrangler Brute pickup has surely had an effect on Jeep's head office, resulting in the company considering building its very own production Wrangler pickup.

Pickup conversions to the Jeep Wrangler have been popular in the US for some years; this is the Brute from American Expedition Vehicles. (Photograph courtesy of AEV)

Modified Wranglers like this Storm model make a nice change from those lucky town dwellers who might otherwise choose a Range Rover. (Photograph courtesy of stuart welford)

US manufacturer Bestop produce clever soft-top options for the Wrangler, but, in the end, it's what you do with your Jeep that really matters.

Modified or standard, your Jeep Wrangler will take you to some special places.

The AEV Brute conversion increases the ability for the Wrangler to carry everything you would need for your adventure. (Photograph courtesy of AEV)

First take your doors off, and then find a desert; this gorgeous copper-coloured Wrangler is from AEV.

The Jeep Wrangler – a can-do off-roader! This version was built using some 4,500 cans of non-perishable food that was donated by the manufacturer to celebrate Canada Day in 2016.

While this aftermarket industry obviously started in the United States, it has quickly grown and become established in Europe, and especially in the UK. The growth of the Internet has helped enthusiasts, and it's now possible to buy pretty much anything you could conceivably want for your Jeep Wrangler at the click of a button.

Ordering from flashy websites is all very well, but for many people it's the seeing, touching and discussing your planned modifications that is all part of the dream to build your very own special Wrangler. The American aftermarket options are huge and today a wide variety of these products are available through official UK suppliers like Nene Overland, Jeepey.com, FTE and G-Force – all experts in all things Jeep, especially the Wrangler. Some people, however, are taking it one step further...

There was a time when 4x4s in the UK were derogatively described as 'Chelsea tractors'. This was before the recent rise in demand for SUVs, since today nearly every manufacturer from Bentley to Fiat has a 4x4 in its product range. One company, however, didn't want to drop the Chelsea tractor moniker and turned the whole thing to its advantage.

Kahn Design produce a whole range of Wrangler specials.

The Kahn Design options are not expected to be taken off-road – these are for the UK's urban jungle!

Hard top or soft-top? It is possible to have the best of both worlds with the Wrangler.

Removing the side doors of a Wrangler does make a difference; this is another Kahn Design special.

Interiors by Kahn Design are an individual bespoke option, with all tastes being catered for.

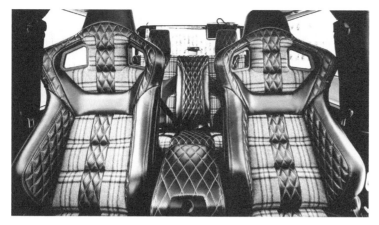

Not for everyone perhaps, but you are unlikely to meet another Wrangler with a similar interior.

The Wrangler does lend itself to the black and red trimming option. Very smart.

Kahn Design proudly displaying its Chelsea Truck Company colours.

Kahn Design produce a range of customised and modified bespoke vehicles for people who want something very different. These are high-quality, high-priced machines, and the company describes itself as 'the world's leading automotive fashion house', which is no idle boast given that they produce customised models from manufacturers like Lamborghini, Ferrari, Rolls-Royce, Land Rover, Range Rover, Mercedes-Benz, Bentley and Aston Martin. Kahn Design also has a subsidiary called the Chelsea Truck Company and it produces some simply amazing Jeep Wrangler models. They are aimed firmly for on-road cruising, and the spectacular interiors do not encourage you to climb aboard wearing muddy wellies, but the sheer opulence and variety of models produced only further confirms the flexibility of the Wrangler.

Jeepey.com is a small family run business. Their range of Wrangler Storms are impressive and very dramatic. (Photograph courtesy of Stuart Walford)

Wrangler Storms can have all the necessary accessories for off-roading, yet you'd suspect that winch seldom gets used. (Photograph courtesy of Stuart Walford)

Lifted, and with those neat 'eyebrow' covers on the headlamps and front grille, this is one mean-looking Wrangler Storm. (Photograph courtesy of Stuart Walford)

Causing a storm, quite literally, are some models produced by one other British company – Jeepey.com. Started by an enthusiast who wanted to produce something different for his family to enjoy, this father and son setup now produce a spectacular range of Storm Jeeps, and if you like your Wranglers to have that tough, brutal appearance, there has to be a Storm model for you.

This flexibility and ability to transform a production vehicle into something very different has much to do with the Jeep Wrangler's enduring success. It's also important to recognise that while many prestige manufacturers are less than pleased when independent companies look to customise their precious production models, believing that their products cannot be improved, Jeep is very different. Throughout its long and mixed ownership, those in charge of the Jeep brand have recognised that such a view is short-sighted; indeed, Jeep has embraced that desire of enthusiasts to build something very personal. Such developments do not undervalue the production vehicle. Rather, they add to it and, as we explain in the next chapter, the manufacturer has also got in on the act with its authorised concept models.

CHAPTER 5

Concept Vehicles: Looking to the Future, and the Past

Proud of its heritage, and yet always wanting to look towards the future, Jeep as a manufacturer has never lost its belief that the company produces vehicles that are born to drive off-road. As a company, it also makes an effort to ensure it remains connected to its owners, and once a year this involves the Easter Jeep Safari, which takes place over the challenging trails of Moab in Utah, USA. These off-road desert trails are now legendary for many off-roaders, and not just Jeep enthusiasts. The desert area around the city of Moab has in the past been the centre of highly lucrative mining operations, originally for uranium and vanadium, but tourism has taken over and those original mining routes are now off-road trails that can be driven. They have marvellous names like Chicken Corners, Secret Spire, Hells Revenge and Poison Spider Mesa; some of the tracks are relatively easy, but some are not (check out the Lion's Back on YouTube to see one trail that is about as difficult as it can get!).

The 2016 Easter Jeep Safari saw thousands of Jeep fans converge on Moab to celebrate the 75th Anniversary of the Jeep brand and the 50th running of the event. The anniversary was celebrated with a range of 75th Anniversary 'specials', including the Wrangler, while at the Safari, Jeep also unveiled its latest range of concept vehicles. These models are designed

Jeep produces a whole range of concept vehicles each year. Besides Wranglers, note the pickup version of the latest Renegade.

The Jeep Treo concept looks more like it's destined to be driven on the moon rather than as a terrestrial vehicle.

The Jeep Willys2 concept incorporates elements of the original Willys Jeep.

As with all official Jeep concepts, the Willys2 was a fully working vehicle.

Produced some years ago, this concept remains surprisingly current. It is more like a modern SUV than a Jeep off-roader.

Hot stuff! This Wrangler has regularly been used to promote someone else's concepts!

This was a very special concept that was shown in 2016 – the Crew Chief 715.

Based on a Wrangler Unlimited, the Crew Chief 715 is fitted with 40-inch military tyres.

and built by a special engineering team known as the Underground Group. These machines use products from the Jeep Performance Parts portfolio, which are available through the company's Mopar accessory arm, and they produce working, driveable concepts of what could be future models, or specials that could be built to meet the demands of the commercial sector, be that for emergency services or for overland expedition, or, just maybe, are built just for the hell of it. These are not 'look-and-don't-touch' concepts that you may see under bright neon lights at an international motor show; these things all work and Jeep listens to the feedback from the Jeep enthusiasts throughout the Safari as they are driven and demonstrated along those famous Moab trails.

The 2016 concepts included one real star of the show, which was the Jeep Crew Chief 715. Built on the base of a Wrangler Unlimited, the Crew Chief reflected the heritage of the Kaiser M715 military service truck. Complete with 20-inch beadlock wheels and massive 40-inch NDT military tyres, the Crew Chief was fitted with the Pentastar V6 engine (used in a number of production line Jeep vehicles).

There was also the 'chopped' Wrangler Shortcut, which was built to reflect the heritage of the original CJ-5 and evoke the spirit of 1950s America. But for pure Wrangler fans, the lime green Trailcat was the concept that most have wanted to take home. Designed as an ultimate off-road machine, it was powered by a massive 6.2 litre HEMI Hellcat V8 engine, which claimed to produce 707 bhp and was mated to a six-speed gearbox. Quite the special Wrangler!

If big is beautiful, then short can be too. This is the Jeep Shortcut, a concept that aimed to evoke the spirit of America in the 1950s.

Even when shortened, there's still room to squeeze in Jeep's 3.6 litre V6 Pentastar engine.

Dwarfed by the desert rocks, the Jeep Shortcut looks almost toy-like.

This looks serious, and with a claimed 707 bhp under the bonnet, you had better believe the Jeep Trailcat is exactly that!

Sitting on massive 39.5-inch BFGoodrich Krawler All Terrain tyres, it's a big step up from a standard Wrangler.

Proving that these Jeep concept vehicles are not all show and no go, the Trailcat cuts up rough.

The Jeep Hurricane was produced in 2005 and is a cross between a Wrangler and a beach buggy!

No doors for the Hurricane, but lots of chrome and the obligatory racing seats.

The amazing thing about the Hurricane concept was its ability to steer all four wheels independently!

These concept vehicles have been produced from the Jeep Underground Group team for a number of years, and there have been some exceptional offerings, many of which we have illustrated here. In particular, the Jeep Hurricane of 2005 was described as the most manoeuvrable Jeep ever produced. Besides having no less than two 5.7 litre HEMI V8 engines, allowing the driver to select four-, eight-, twelve- or sixteen-cylinders, depending on the needs, it also had a mechanically controlled four-wheel torque distribution system, allowing for different amounts of power to be directed to different wheels. This is a real benefit to off-road driving when different wheels may have different grip and traction depending on the terrain being driven through. Perhaps the oddest thing about the Hurricane was the ability for each of the four wheels to turn in on itself and allow the vehicle to spin as if on a turntable; this facility actually allowed the driver to move sideways without changing the direction the vehicle is pointing.

The Jeep Switchback is packed with Mopar and Jeep Performance Parts, including bizarre open-air doors!

The Trailstorm concept has just the right paintwork to ensure the Jeep merges into the desert landscape.

The Jeep Switchback is designed to appeal to 'techies', with an iPad on the dashboard and rotating rear seats.

Truly American, the Jeep Quicksand is obviously a hot-rod-inspired Wrangler, and looks great!

One star of the 2017 Jeep Easter Safari was the Luminator; check out the row of LED lights on the bonnet.

Above: The Jeep concepts take to the Moab trails – does off-roading get any better than this?

Left: While the concept Jeeps look forward, there's never a moment when the heritage is forgotten.

A lightweight expedition Wrangler; note the drone neatly fitted to the Jeep's roof.

The complete 2016 Jeep 75th Anniversary range: Wrangler, Renegade, Grand Cherokee and Cherokee.

Jeep has also investigated the benefits of an electric Wrangler, but we perhaps need battery technology to advance considerably before that will succeed for an off-roader (there aren't many places to plug in if you are travelling off-road). However, while the company supports the work from the boys in the Underground, the future of the Jeep product, and the Wrangler in particular, looks to be in safe – and exciting – hands.

The Wrangler Level Red is so named as that represents the highest level of difficulty any Moab trail can be awarded – and this Jeep would cope.

Some colours just suit Wranglers and this has to be the sort of desert Wrangler you would want to own.

This shot clearly demonstrates that even the concept vehicles keep the Wrangler's impressive four-wheel articulation.

The Jeep CJ66 concept is based on a TJ chassis, and is adorned with a 1966 CJ shaped body.

From the rear, the influence of the CJ models is obvious on the CJ66 concept.

The future Wrangler? Will we ever see a production-based electric Wrangler?

A hybrid Wrangler concept with a smaller engine still fitted, but supported by electric motors.

Even in its 'ev' Jeep concept mode, this is obviously a Wrangler.

CHAPTER 6

Buy It, Use It: The Best Way to Enjoy the Wrangler

While we obviously hope you have enjoyed browsing through this book, and have even perhaps learned something new about the Jeep Wrangler, for some, this is just the start. There's one more step to take. It's certainly a great story, and a tribute to a vehicle that started life in such difficult circumstances and yet has continued, under a number of different owners, to remain a much-loved, iconic off-roader. But for real fans, there is only one way to truly enjoy the Wrangler, and that's to own one – and take it off-road.

The UK is awash with SUVs these days, and while those initials are supposed to represent Sports Utility Vehicle and thereby give the vehicle that extra ingredient of being sporty and fun, as well as being a vehicle that can enthuse the enthusiast, most of them, let's face it, don't. Most of them are dull, if practical, with the only sporty ingredient being the ability to take the kids to the park.

But the Jeep Wrangler is different. While it is a vehicle that you could use for everyday transport, supermarket visits and school runs, it does have some limitations when it comes to creature comforts and luggage space. However, if you want a Wrangler to be special and give you the chance for adventure, then you should dive into the market and find yourself one.

Looking to buy a Wrangler? Then the 4.0 litre Sport version is a great place to start.

One of the first official advertisements, which was aimed at getting civilians to buy the new CJ models.

Versatility was the key with the Jeep, as it remains today, but this early advertisement aims it as a working vehicle.

As you can read elsewhere in the book, there have been a variety of Wranglers over the years, and so it pays to make a decision to focus on exactly what you want. Looking for an original Willys or Ford Jeep, or even the CJ models, is a specialist area, and not really something we have the space to cover here. If you just want a Wrangler for its on-road presence – and there's nothing wrong with that, especially with 'jelly mould' SUVs all looking the same these days – then the first Wrangler, the YJ, could be ideal. It's not the best if you want to go off-road, but the designs of that era – especially those loud graphics that are often found on the bonnet – makes this a model you're certain to be seen in! The latest JK models offer the best of both worlds; the creature comforts have much improved, yet it will still take you into the rough stuff. For the true enthusiast, however, it probably has to be the TJ models, built between 1996 and 2006, that will draw your attention.

Above: Always check that a Wrangler fitted with the removable hardtop is indeed removable; once off, they can be very difficult to get back on.

Left: Even in standard format, like this TJ version, the Wrangler has impressive rock climbing abilities.

The Wrangler TJ Sahara has a few more luxuries than the more basic Sport version.

Your options when buying a TJ will be whether to go for a 2.5 litre or 4.0 litre engine.

If you are looking for a TJ, the first decision has to be on the engine front, since your choice will be either the 2.5 litre four-cylinder or the 4.0 litre straight-six in the UK. The smaller version is a reliable enough unit, so if it has been regularly serviced, all should be OK. However, the Wrangler is quite a heavy vehicle and so the engine may have had a hard life; listen for any nasty rattling from the bottom end as this could imply worn bearings. Grey exhaust smoke and noises from the top can hint at excessive cylinder wear. Do check which model 2.5 litre you have as the very early engines into the UK only had 117 bhp, which, to be frank, isn't enough. After 2001, the uprated engines produced 140 bhp, which is certainly better, but this smaller engine doesn't really have enough torque to cope with any serious off-roading. It is a tough unit though, and if it's been treated well it should be good for around 200,000 miles before needing a serious rebuild.

The real TJ choice has to be to get a Wrangler with the 4.0 litre engine. Interestingly, you probably won't notice much of a difference in fuel consumption between the two units in real life. Yes, the smaller engine is theoretically more economical, but since it is less powerful, the tendency is to drive it harder, thereby consuming more fuel. The larger engine has a claimed 174 bhp and a much higher torque figure of 218 pound-feet, and can lead to you driving in a much more 'laid back' manner; you will probably still use a little more fuel, but you'll enjoy doing it.

The majority of models available in the UK are likely to have the three-speed automatic engine option, but it could be worth searching out the rarer four-speed; although, if you intend to take your Wrangler off-road, then manual is a better option (it might also take the edge off the fuel consumption figure). Towards the very end of the TJ's run, the five-speed manual was replaced with a six-speed. This won't make much of a difference off-road, but will be better if you plan to do some motorway journeys as well.

Equipment-wise, the TJ is relatively basic. The Sport is the base version and if original could very well just have a two-speaker, simple ICE system. Of course, many owners will have fitted their own aftermarket systems, which may include speakers fitted to the integral roll bar. Sahara models have air conditioning, cruise control and a much better, original ICE system.

The most difficult aspect of buying a Wrangler comes when it has had any significant mechanical modifications – especially a suspension lift. A true enthusiast will go into great details about what they have done, or, more importantly, who did the conversion. This will allow you to check with the specialist involved to make sure everything was done properly.

If you have never driven a lifted 4x4 before, don't be too alarmed when on the road. Just remember that this is not a sports car! It will be when you take the lifted Wrangler off into the mud that you will get the full benefit. Tyres will make a big difference here and for some, having two sets is the best option; one set being suitable for the tarmac and then more serious rubber for use off-road. If may be obvious, but it is worth noting that 'knobbly' off-road tyres will not offer you the same grip on the tarmac as you might be used to. As ever, it's a case of driving accordingly.

There shouldn't be any squeaks and groans from the steering, and if you hear this it could mean a problem with the power steering pump. While accepting the steering won't be as precise as you might be used to, vague steering or excessive kickback could just mean problems from worn ball joints or the need to replace the steering damper. Take time checking this out if you know the car has spent a lot of time off-road.

Do have a look under any Wrangler you may consider buying and check for off-road damage and/or corrosion to the ladder-frame chassis. Buying a vehicle with a long MOT is the best option, as with any vehicle. You probably want the Wrangler for some open-topped fun; however, if it comes with a hardtop, make sure that all the necessary fittings are there as an ill-fitting top will mean unpleasant wind noise and possible water leaks. If you get a well-fitting soft-top, count yourself lucky. Even when new these are not the easiest to take off and put back on – but that's all part of the fun! Remember that when you are trying to pull the rear zipper securing the rear screen...

The Australian Old Man Emu company has a fine reputation for uprated Wrangler suspension options.

Terraflex suspension upgrades are now available in the UK and are designed specifically for the TJ Wrangler.

Now that's what you call axle articulation! Rubicon Express offer long-arm suspension upgrades, making a Wrangler virtually unstoppable.

You must also check that your Wrangler will go from on-road two-wheel drive, into four-wheel drive and low range. From experience, it's fair to say that slotting the small lever into low range can sometimes be something of a struggle, so don't worry if that's the case. Just make sure you can actually select 4x4, as that is the real reason you are buying it.

If you buy a vehicle and intend to modify it yourself, then enjoy! There are a lot of companies out there who can offer help and assistance. From our experience, suspension kits from the US firm Terraflex and the famous Australian company Old Man Emu should be considered. If you are really serious and looking for a 5.5 inch lift, then check out what's on offer from Rubicon Express; they have all the bits to make your Wrangler unstoppable.

Going Off-Road

There are numerous places across the UK where you can take your 4x4 off-road, which are often referred to as Pay 'n' Play sites. The terrain and facilities do vary, hugely, but if you want to get to know exactly how to drive your Wrangler, then it could make sense to visit the official Jeep Off-Road Driving Centre. This is based at the Carden Park Hotel, Cheshire (www.4x4eventsuk.co.uk). The instructors here are a talented and friendly bunch and you will get to drive the very latest Wrangler over some interesting and challenging terrain. There's also the option to drive the full Jeep range, so be careful as you might end up spending more than you bargained for. Getting expert tuition before you go it alone makes a lot of sense, and these guys are true Jeep enthusiasts, so it's worth a visit.

One thing you should certainly budget for when buying a Jeep Wrangler is the annual membership fee to the Jeep Owners Club (www.jeepowners.club). This is a vibrant and friendly club that organises a whole host of events across the UK and overseas. There should be something there for all Wrangler owners. You also have the benefit of a group of people who probably know the answers to any technical issues you may have. The club is affiliated to other Jeep clubs around the world, and as such is recognised by the manufacturer. They have off-road days, often with driver instruction, social meetings, greenlane trips and some serious expedition trips where you can really take your Wrangler into the wild. It's a must, really.

But that's the thing about the Wrangler. You are buying more than just an off-road vehicle, you are buying a lifestyle, a hobby and a link to a motoring heritage that goes back over seventy-five years. You are buying an iconic 4x4. Enjoy it!

The Wrangler Unlimited won *4x4 Magazine's* 2017 Hardcore Class in the annual 4x4 Of The Year contest.

Mud, glorious mud, and the delights of taking the Jeep Wrangler off-road; car and driver are in perfect harmony. (Photograph courtesy of Wayne Mitchelson)

Off-road trialling is a challenging and highly addictive sport. Join a local off-road club and try it yourself. (Photograph courtesy of Toby Savage)

Pay 'n' Play sites allow you to enjoy your Wrangler in ideal conditions. You'll probably need to clean it afterwards before returning to the public roads.

At speed across muddy rough terrain, the Wrangler Unlimited makes an imposing sight.

Born to be Free; Jeep and Harley-Davidson often join forces for marketing and sales promotions.

This 2016 Wrangler is fitted with the 2.8 litre CRD engine; it is full of torque and great off-road.

If you want some proper tuition, take an off-road driving course. Here a 'spotter' is guiding the driver over a log bridge. (Photograph courtesy of Wayne Mitchelson)

Slippery log obstacles need care and the smooth use of the throttle, but it's something the Wrangler can do with ease. (Photograph courtesy of Wayne Mitchelson)

Above: Jeep has its own off-road test ground at Balocco in Italy. Much of it is man-made to demonstrate the vehicle's off-road abilities.

Right: The Italian Job; thanks to Jeep's Fiat ownership, the manufacturer has sponsored top Italian football team, Juventus, who appear to have gotten very muddy for this posed advertising picture!

Above: Wherever they are built, or driven, the Jeep will always be an all-American vehicle.

Left: No matter what new models are produced, older models will always find their way onto the Jeep show stand.